How Pleasant It Is

Neal Whitman

ISBN: 978-93-89690-75-0

First Edition: 2020
Rs. 200/-

Cyberwit.net
HIG 45 Kaushambi Kunj, Kalindipuram
Allahabad - 211011 (U.P.) India
http://www.cyberwit.net
Tel: +(91) 9415091004 +(91) (532) 2552257
E-mail: info@cyberwit.net

Printed at Repro India Limited.

From This Moment On Paperback – February 18, 2020

by Neal Whitman (Author)

Paperback: 66 pages
Publisher: Cyberwit.net (February 18, 2020)
Language: English
ISBN-10: 9389690382
ISBN-13: 978-9389690385

The haiku reveal elegance, good taste and clarity of thought. All haiku show strong inspiration and create a lyricism of striking appeal and power.

To Amelia Fielden and Edwin A. Cranston

May I add appreciation to my wife, Elaine, for the cover photograph of a saké cup that sits on a shelf above the desk where I write poetry. This piece was made by the poet who came to be known as Rengetsu (1791 - 1875), which means "Lotus Moon." The calligraphy and waka (tanka) was hers.

koki mazeshi
haru no nishiki no
monaka yori
nioi idetaru
uguisu no koe

from the midst of
the spring splendor of
mixed blossoms
comes the fragrance of
the bush warbler singing

Preface

some say
the split between earth and sky
is real, others not –
some accept dogma and know it
others do, but don't know it

Look at our book shelves. I am a "lumper" and my books are stacked horizontally and vertically. My wife is a "splitter" - poetry on a high shelf, prose on low.

Ribbons, Tanka Cafe feature
spring/summer 2012

It is said that there are two types of people: those who say there are two types of people and those who do not. From my tanka above and its prose note, you know how I see it.

So, when it comes to New Year's Resolutions, it will not surprise you that I think there are two types of people: those who make them and those who do not! I happen to be the type who does not make New Year's Resolutions … except … I did …twice… each time "tanka-related".

First, I made a resolution on January 1, 2011, to learn how to write tanka. I had been writing general poetry since 2005 and haiku since 2008. By the way, there are two types of people who make New Year's Resolutions: those who keep 'em and those who don't. I kept that one! I did so by reading, reading, and more reading.

The first journal editor who accepted my tanka in a journal was Amelia Fielden who was the guest editor for the summer 2011 issue of *Simply Haiku*. For me it was Kismet because she was one of the poets whose tanka I had been reading. It is said that good poems make good teachers. I discovered that her tanka were *master* teachers. Thus, she is one of the two dedicatees for this collection of my tanka.

Second, I made a resolution on January 1, 2020, to start and finish by the end of the year a 988-page book: *A Waka Anthology, Volume One: The Gem-Glistening Cup* translated and edited by Edwin A. Cranston. Edwin is a Professor of Japanese literature in the Department of East Asian Languages and Cultures at Harvard University whose primary research interest is the classical literature of Japan, including waka, a traditional form we now call tanka.

Elaine and I became friends with Edwin and his wife, Fumiko, over the several years when the two of them attended the annual Robinson Jeffers Fall Festival in Carmel, California. How pleasant it was to share with them the festival's traditional Sunday morning poetry walk on Carmel Beach. Edwin is the second dedicatee of this book … may I add that, at the time of publication of this short collection of my tanka, progress I am making in reading his long anthology bodes well for my keeping this resolution.

Whether or not you make New Year's Resolutions, I wish you in this Year 2020 the touchstone of clear vision. It need not require new eye glasses to see clarity in poetry. I hope you find it in mine. A bonus for me would be to learn that it is pleasing … and pleasant!

The title of this book, like its opening tanka sequence, was inspired by the Japanese poet and classical scholar at the end of the Edo period, Tachibana Akemi (1812 - 1868), who wrote 52 poems that begin with the phrase, *tanoshimi wa*, "how pleasant it is."

Though highly respected in Japan, the work of Tachibana gained world-wider audience when in 1994 President Bill Clinton quoted the poet as he welcomed Emperor Akihito and Empress Michiko to the White House with these words:

Let us listen to the elegant words left to us by the Japanese poet, Tachibana Akemi: "It is a pleasure when, rising in the morning, I go outside and find a flower that has bloomed that was not there yesterday."

That verse is more than a century old, but its message is timeless. Every day brings with it the promise of a new blossom: the prospect of progress and growing friendship between our two peoples.

My tanka are mostly in chronological order, but sometimes out of sequence when I thought a pairing would be more pleasing. How pleasant it is for me that you hold this book in your hands. My hope is that the feeling is mutual.

how pleasant it is

how pleasant it is —
to see in my postal box
a letter
from an old friend ...
old in both senses

how pleasant it is —
to hear bird chatter
when I wake ...
The Avian Network
broadcasts only good news

how pleasant it is —
to smell long stem roses
she arranges
in the art nouveau vase
we found in a yard sale

how pleasant it is —
to taste a hint of sage
in the *coq au vin*
that has been simmering
in a cast iron cocotte

how pleasant it is —
to touch the smooth stone
in my pocket
as I recite the poem
that also came home with me

International Tanka No. 6, 2019

slats in the lattice fence
crisscross diagonally
in diamond-shaped spaces
two vines intertwine
jasmine and morning glory
Simply Haiku, Summer 2011

the barn window
lit by a source
unknown to me
this evening
I read Thomas Hardy
Simply Haiku, Summer 2011

one dram of whisky
with a drop of sea water
Jura's Superstition*
provokes the illusion
of Big Sur fog
Ribbons, Fall 2011

* malt touted as bold, strong, and peated

white space
around and between sounds
I hear a muffled *brooo-brooo*
snowshoeing at twilight
there – a tundra ghost – maybe
Atlas Poetica, Winter 2011

overripe
persimmons, plums, and pears
in a bowl
beside the brushes and paint
I laid out last week

Simply Haiku, Fall 2011

a young man and his dog
both sleeping on a park bench
with one buck in his hat –
an "old hand" saunters past
and lifts hat . . . and bill!

Atlas Poetica, "Social Realism" 2011

back and forth
a dredger in the harbor
clears a clogged channel
my sister's confession:
he hits me
Atlas Poetica, Winter 2011

"Get off my rock."
a glaucous gull who could talk
in his beak a deed
though it looked to me like
someone's old laundry list
Atlas Poetica, Winter 2011

the boat dock
splintered silvery green –
a mallard paddling by
leaves behind
one white feather
Magnapoets, December 2011

Be Silent, Be Still
retreat rules here are few –
I pick up lentil soup
in the communal kitchen
and return with solitude
Magnapoets, December 2011

at a loss
to know what to do
my first artichoke
dripping hollandaise sauce
on her white lace linen
    Multiverses, Spring 2012

on the plaza
before the concert begins
rain showers
and a sprinkle of twigs
dropped by nesting crows
    Notes from the Gean, June 2012

a heckuva storm
I hear the distress signal
of the steamboat
now that I am connoisseur
of natural catastrophe
Atlas Poetica, Summer 2012

winter soon when
days turns to night suddenly
I prefer autumn
when afternoon skies are streaky
and dusk drops slowly
Ribbons, Fall 2012

one foot past the sign
No Fishing Beyond This Point!
she plants her big butt –
this woman casts her line
and makes a statement
Atlas Poetica, Summer 2012

in Yosemite
he is locked in the outhouse
this stinks
it took a booted kick
for the old coot to bust his way out
Atlas Poetica, March 2013

stifling hot
a score of railcars rolls by
a boy scout salutes
I'm watching, watching, watching
So long Bobby
    Ribbons, Winter 2012

his after-life
like his before-life
filled with unknowns
not to witness the births
of his grandson and grandfather
    Ribbons, Spring-Summer 2013

my old crowd
was absent from our hangout
I raised one finger –
"Black Jack, water back …
make it a double."
Atlas Poetica, July 2013

dogs on the beach
happy to see other dogs –
at the airport
how much I detest
all those other people
Kernels, Summer 2013

one summer morning
the circus came to town
by nightfall
my best friend and I made plans
how we could join the troupe
Diogen Pro Kultura Magazin, 2013
First Prize Summer Tanka

waiting on the dock
a woman holds a placard
with my name on it
I am put in her arms,
my mother singing to me
Eucalypt 15, 2013
Distinctive Scribbling Award

a boy baits his hook
and with a quick wrist snap
off he flies
now floating on the pond
Cricket at the end of his line

labeled “As Is”
a ceramic cricket cage
with a cracked lid
its laughing fisherman
knows what I should offer

Diogen Pro Kultura Magazin, 2013
both tanka awarded Best Autumn Tanka

here, maybe
in the snow squall
a white kimono
wind whipping through the aspens …
or Yuki-onna's icy breath

Atlas Poetica, "All Hallow's Evening: Supernatural Tanka 2013

*for Geraldine Books**
a dipping sun
my limbs had grown heavy
I was mortified
all I had done that day
had gone ill

Poems Found In March, 2013

**Found Poetry Review* sponsored a project, Pulitzer Remix, which invited poets to "find" lines in books that had won the Pulitzer Prize for Fiction. I was assigned *March* by Geraldine Brooks. This novel tells the story of John March, the father in the family Louisa May Alcott introduced us to in *Little Women*. In this poem, I took lines from the pages of my birth date: 3, 27,19, 48.

two more tanka "found" in *March* by Geraldine Brooks …

fog stood thick –
feasting on berries
my mood was elevated
reading poetry in the cool afternoon
though the opening door

rolling
the river fast flowing
rising water
sparkle shimmer river
currents swept swift

"It's not a mountain,"
my hospice client tells me,
"it's a desert."
he places in my hand
a Tuareg* amulet
Ribbons, Spring-Summer 2014

*a nomadic pastoral people who live in the Sahara Desert

her lab tests are in
Will the news be good or bad?
mare's tail overhead
this blue sky is deceptive
it's a sign of a storm front
All the Shells, Tanka Society of America Anthology, 2014

on its first flight
you should have seen how my kite
flew higher than gulls
the wind blew from land to sea
the string snapped and off she went
Diogen Pro Kultura Magazin, 2014
Second Prize, Spring Tanka

my poetry group
gathers at the park terrace
rain-blessed leaves
transform the concrete surface
into a Greek mosaic
cattails, September 2014
Pen the Painting prize

parachute lessons
for my 65th birthday
What was I thinking?
I put the bucket list book
in the thrift shop pile
Ribbons, Fall 2014

Art Deco cufflinks
for my sixty-sixth birthday
stunning though these are
my fingers are not quite right
to lock them in place
Eucalypt 16, 2014

fog stands thick
spotted atop a plum thistle
a male bunting
a camera is of no use
when the spot of paint flies off

The Tanka Journal, Nihon Kajin Club 45, 2014

fog stands thick
Una* scans their poetry shelf
Yeats trumps Hardy
her voice rises and falls
in rhythm with the ebb tide

Kigo: Seaonal Words, Summer 2014 Chuff Books

*Una Jeffers, wife of poet Robinson Jeffers, was known to recite poetry in their Tor House stone cottage. In 1950 she died of breast cancer.

on the cancer wing
visitors have long gone home
dimmed lights
at the nurses' station –
he tells them a knock-knock joke
Eucalypt 17, 2014

before I knock
I take my own pulse
then let myself in –
her heart stent is not
just a metaphor for life
Iris International (Ivanic Grad, Croatia), 2015

attar of roses
was I still in dreamland
or was I awake?
each one of my senses
has its own alarm clock

The Tanka Journal, Nihon Kajin Club 46, 2015

on the Self-Help shelf,
next to *Dating for Dummies,*
Dating Old Photographs
I put it back in Antiques
and move on to Poetry

Out of Sequence, ed. D. Gilson, Anderson, SC: Parlor Press, 2015

yes, no, maybe
I try to stay open to new ideas
three sides
... of land surround the bay
... of water surround the headland
Eucalypt 19, 2015

in the uncertain hour
no longer night, but not yet day
between drip and drop
shadows are sharp and intense
between being and un-being
Ribbons, Winter 2015

in the museum
photos of Fukushima
after the earthquake
a boy asks his father
what made the sky fall down?
Ribbons, Winter 2015

"the verdancy rose"
not the Garden of Eden
Hiroshima
John Hersey's vivid account
biblical in proportion
Atlas Poetica, "The Atomic Era – 70 Years of…" 2015

a lovely sea bird
dips her wing into the wave
we drop anchor
rising from the spindrift
a rainbow leaves us too soon
cattails, Fall 2015
first honorable mention, Fleeting Words

all marvel
sea stars and jellyfish rise
out of the ocean
now floating above us
bioluminescence
The Tanka Journal, Nihon Kajin Club 48, 2016

chattering
kokako and keruru
two mugs
not our faces … ceramics
we toast our Kiwi friend
Kokako 23, 2015

in her bequest
my mother's toby jug
missing one arm
I pick up the telephone
and call my estranged brother
Eucalypt 20, 2016

for flowers
Anonymous money sent
to the nursing home
she folded the envelope
into iris origami
Gusts 21, Spring/Summer 2015

a King and pawn
return to the same wood box
when I was young
I relied on the opening
but now it's the end game
Skylark, Winter 2015

he tells me
his sense of falling has ceased
he is flying –
at a hospice visit
I learn to suspend judgement
Gusts 21, Fall/Winter 2014

in my hospice work
I learn a portmanteau word
gremorse
grief for what has been lost
remorse for what should have been
Kokako 23, 2015

she was coming in
as I was on my way out
I had not known
we shared the same doctor
or that now she would be bald
Gusts 21, Spring/Summer 2015

it's called *Slow TV*
12 hours of Aran knitting
Norwegians love it –
now that it has gone world-wide
I can watch firewood burn
Skylark, Winter 2015

seven spoons
fill a jelly jar on our mantle
each one
reminds us to stir sweetness
into each day of the week
Atlas Poetica, "I'll Be Home" 2015

early morning
is a time of magic
the street is silent
after the light has come
before the sun has risen
The Tanka Journal, Nihon Kajin Club 47, 2015

our passion for peace
erases man-made map lines
no more boundaries
the Earth is a spinning top
but need not be a blur

Eucalypt 20, 2016

on edge
no need for a compass
no false borders
we let go of destinations
with faith in faith

Immagine e Poesia, Torino, Italy e-book 2016

her whole life
was a game of hopscotch –
harder at seventy
to hop from square to square
without stepping on lines

Ripples in the Sand, Tanka Society of America anthology 2016

who invented
the rectangular grid?
not raccoons
but bandits running roughshod
over our common ground

Earth: Our Common Ground, selected and arranged by Claire Everett, 2017

added to the bliss
of a sandalwood candle
is its care-taking
she knew how to trim a wick
to make the light last longer
Skylark, Winter 2016

the widow next door
plays the *Moonlight Sonata*
on a spinet
as Beethoven composed it –
no self-pity or remorse
Skylark, Winter 2016

more like a mirror
less like an open window
when I read Jung –
I skip my friend's funeral
and play Elgar's *Nimrod*

Ribbons, Fall 2016

on my bedstead
I keep a pencil and pad
up once to pee
the sun rises on my notes:
sea turtles dream they can fly

Certificate of Merit, Fine Work, Japan Tanka Poets' Society, 2016

I "found" these two tanka in *Death Comes for the Archbishop* by Willa Cather (1927). Both tanka are told from the point of view of *Angelica* and *Contento*, the two mules that carried Archbishop Latour and Vicar Apostolic Vaillant across the rugged landscape of New Mexico following its annexation by the United States.

are we born this way?
they say a mule is stubborn
a man of faith
would say he is steadfast –
my doubt is broad and deep

night closes
rain as heavy as ever
I feel the trust
as my man accepts my lead
Angelica and I find Mora*

Bearing the Mask: Southwestern Persona Poems, edited by Scott Wiggerman and Cindy Huyser. Albuquerque: Dos Gatos Press, 2016

*The Archbishop and Vicar were traveling to a remote village, Mora, to help the local *padre* care for a group of destitute refugees.

when I cannot sleep
I picture Uncle Vanya
snoozing on stage
perhaps I'm that actor
pretending to be asleep
Gusts 23, Spring/Summer 2016

my English teacher
did his darn best to ruin
Joseph Conrad
Ships … Ships are all right.
It's the men in them.
Gusts 23, Spring/Summer 2016

a lion
a woman and a mandolin
under the moon
rumors of warm daybreak
Gypsy music in a dream
    Bay Area Poets Coalition, honorable mention 2017

at age twelve
I read *The Martian Chronicles* –
staring
at myself in the mirror
I detected pointy ears
    red lights, Summer 2017

Mom had read
the "sleepy-song" poem
to me at bedtime –
now her granddaughter recites it
by heart at her Nana's wake
red lights, Summer 2017

the road to our home
used to be a bumpy ride
newly paved
the sign still says SLOW DOWN
Come, let's watch the tide go out!
red lights, Summer 2017

Rinpoche
dings the singing bowl –
where had I gone?
and where did the last
wisp of incense go?
International Tanka, Summer 2017

light a wooden match
and then … whoosh … blow it out
where did the light go?
I'm no Einstein, but I think
the flame stretched invisibly thin
International Tanka, Summer 2017

mini rainbows
appear when the wind blows
across spindrift –
a poet-pal in Japan
emails that she sees this, too

International Tanka, Summer 2017

embroidery
can decorate or bind
slippers
once made for a Mongol bride
now displayed behind glass

The Right Touch of Sun, Tanka Society of America anthology 2017

their love notes
always folded in half
*somonka**
he waited for the ink to dry,
but her letters arrived smudged
Kokako 27, 2017

*tanka letters exchanged between lovers

she loves me
she loves me not
she loves me
no one special on my mind
dull days and summer doldrums
Ribbons, Spring/Summer 2017

Big News!
What's the flap all about?
Monarch butterflies
arrived in Pacific Grove –
"America's Last Home Town"
Brevities: A Mini-Mag of Minimalist Poems 174, 2017

short-term renter
next door to our bungalow
is adamant
she will leave the garden
better than she found it
Atlas Poetica 30, 2017

at night
Moon does not reflect the day
but rises to rule
I am a Lunatic
whose poems arrive in dreams

Life in Pacific Grove, California, edited by Patricia Hamilton, 2017.

by dawn's early light
a black oystercatcher
piping
I march to my own drummer
unseen harbor seals barking

Life in Pacific Grove, California, edited by Patricia Hamilton, 2017.

Violette
in her opera box
perfumed
bouquet of camellias
l'impulso dell'amore
    Immagine e Poesia, October 16, 2017

a street poet
tells me he bleeds in ink
Is that why
dark red lines are visible
in the Balearic Sea?
    Ars Artium 6, January 2018

sushi bar patrons
watch Sumo wrestling
TV on mute –
I order blowfish stew
and wake up dead

Voices: The Art and Science of Psychotherapy, Winter 2018

it's the opposite
of eating potato chips –
once I stopped watching
TV cable news shows
I could not tune in again

Voices: The Art and Science of Psychotherapy, Winter 2018

at the tip
of a blade of grass
a dew drop –
I took out my sketch pad
but it evaporated
Ribbons, Fall 2018

lights out . . .
our summer camp counselor
tells us
goblins hide behind dark clouds –
I've spent a lifetime looking
Ribbons, Fall 2018

through the glade
a girl in a kimono –
komorebi
untranslatable, sunshine
that filters through the leaves
Gusts 28, Fall/Winter 2018

she doused the fire
the fire in my heart
oops, I meant "hearth"
do my typo errors
spell what I really mean?
haigaonline, haiga with Pris Campbell, 2018

Winter Solstice
the sun has gone down elsewhere
where birds sing –
at teatime a reading lamp
signals our concession
Ribbons, Winter 2018

New Year's Day brunch
sharing my first draft tanka
breaks the ice –
our guests make resolutions
to sharpen their pencils, too
Ribbons, Winter 2018

a steady breeze
and aspens newly leafed
murmur secrets –
the two of us stop talking
out of breath on the ascent
Ribbons, Spring / Summer 2018

in a blink
he believes her every word –
a steel guitar
strums in the alleyway
behind the beachside bistro
Eucalypt 25, 2019

his first words
I am so very happy!
always
our monk says meditation
is medicine for the mind
Kokako 28, 2018

the hour is up
but our monk remains seated
he smiles
we smile in return –
no one wants to leave first
Atlas Poetica 36, 2019

the oldest thing
I own is an overcoat …
perhaps
it's time to downsize
because of shrinkage
Kokako 30, 2019

James Joyce tells us
the past is in the present –
we live with ghosts
of our making, shades
of the living and the dead
Kokako 30, 2019

Our Town
Thornton Wilder's prized drama
is a reminder –
realize life while we live it
who does? maybe poets
Poets Salon, hosted by Kath Bela Wilson, March 20, 2019

filtered light
moves through whispering pines –
Chekhov can see
the red glow of sunset
down the path and past our world
red lights, June 2019

wishful thinking
that long ago I would find
a touchstone –
today crossing a bridge
it was right beneath me
    red lights, June 2019

a ship can reckon
our Point Pinos Lighthouse beam
17 miles off shore –
at 12° above NNW
it also can spot the ISS*
    Atlas Poetica 38, 2019

* From the Point Pinos Lighthouse, volunteer docents observed the International Space Station pass over at 8:18 p.m., PST, April 7, 2019. The lighthouse beam is visible up to 17 miles.

with GPS ships
no need for our lighthouse –
now automated
the sweep of Point Pinos beam
counts of unnumbered gulls
Tanka Origins No. 1, August 2019

gusting winds
at Point Pinos Lighthouse –
only hardy souls
venture out to visit …
and maybe a child's ghost
Eucalypt 26, 2019

mountain valley
low lying wild thyme sways
of its own accord –
undercover life of plants
is a secret worth keeping

Vistas of the West, edited by Larry Kapustka et al., 2019

loons
land on the lake
and laugh –
so smooth, not even
a ripple or a wrinkle

Vistas of the West, edited by Larry Kapustka et al., 2019

for DVR
at last
forsythia
signals the start of spring –
my friend also blooms at her door:
"Come in!"
Iris International (Ivanic Grad, Croatia), 2019

Hugo's bellringer
of Notre Dame Cathedral*
lives in harmony –
peopled by marble figures
who can say who is cracked?
Gusts, Fall/Winter 2019

*on April 17, 2019, a massive fire damaged large parts of this icon of Western civilization

reading Robert Frost
now that my hair is white, too –
two roads that diverged
now I see were worn the same …
my teacher had it all wrong
International Tanka No. 4, 2018

“Frost at Midnight”
a fine poem by Coleridge
but for winter warmth
I prefer “Fire and Ice”,
his hair a drift of snow
Ribbons, Winter 2019

she leaves a lamp on
when I go out for a night walk
it's understood
this is a place of peace …
warm and restful inside
Atlas Poetica 36, 2019

what does it mean
to be a non-believer?
I know for a fact
that when the power goes out
it is only the wind
Atlas Poetica 36, 2019

remembering
Fall of the Berlin Wall
thirty years ago*
a mythical moment
Beethoven's *Ode to Joy*
Gusts, Fall/Winter 2019

*November 9, 1989

full-fledged
sprung from the brow of Zeus
Athena the Owl
half mythical, half miracle
my verse
Iris International (Ivanic Grad, Croatia), 2019

pernambuco
the premium choice
for cello bows
my pencil of the same wood
also vibrates, but in verse
Eucalypt 27, 2019

my studio box
of Derwent colour pencils
offers two reds
Scarlet Lake and Crimson Lake
one for Loss, one for Healing
red lights, January 2020

Holst's *Country Song*
transcribed for the pipe organ
heard in the distance –
walking to Wells Cathedral
our tour guide stopped talking

One Man's Maple Moon, sponsored by Chou-en Liu, 2020

sitting still
on a bench by the bay
we watch the sun set
There! a green spot in a sec –
still sitting

International Tanka No. 6, 2020

www.ingramcontent.com/pod-product-compliance
Lightning Source LLC
LaVergne TN
LVHW091231150826
845673LV00003B/1088

* 9 7 8 9 3 8 9 6 9 0 7 5 0 *